The Poems

Hugh Barnes-Yallowley

ISBN   9781542901918

Published by Hugh Barnes-Yallowley

Cover Painting: "A Downland View" by Hugh Barnes-Yallowley

INDEX

Of Death, and Life

When all was white with frost,
And Yuletide had come'
The Lord called
And he came
For his Earth's work was done.

In cloak of silent night,
With air cold and chill'
A man was
Born to Live
As Jesus said we will.

Thus weep not for the dead
But for the living cry
The dead Live
Leaving us,
The living still to die.

Purley
December 1944

5

Is Every Bee attracted by Scent?

All things must grow old,
Of this is my story told;
For I'm sorry for the trees,
The Trees who still bear leaves,
But now the leaves of ivy
Or some other parasitic plant.

As the tree grows old,
The ivy takes her hold;
 a cov'ring mass,
Without which he must crash,
But if the truth be told
His soul has already crashed.

She sucks his sap away,
She is come forever to stay,
For now he cannot resist
As she can always insist;
And when his soul is gone,
She'll live in a saprophytic way.

December 1944

6

"To build castle in the air is to make a fool's paradise"

O to look upon the highest peek
Where the snow lies cool,
Still to look for distant lands
And to be a fool!
O to be a fool and seek
For a land unknown,
O to look on starry heights
And a golden throne.
O to live in ecstasy,
And to dream one's dreams
O to see the golden age
And to live, … it seems, ..
As the happiest man alive
Without a worry or care –
But the happiest man alive
Has always a load to bear;
For thro' work he's reached his goal
And not be wishing long
For the joy he hopes to have
And the "World of Song"
"The World of Song" that in the eyes
Of those who see aright
Is far from coming while men seek
In the dead of night –
Without the sense to turn to God
The "One Almighty Light"

March 1945

7

"London's lonely, as the country's homely"

As a leaf, I wander lone
Blown by an autumn breeze,
Blown along the cold grey stone
Of a city street, I freeze.
I freeze for the lack of a friend
The lack of a firm handshake
I feel as though my way I wend
Adrift on an unknown lake.
I am alone, yet in mass,
Of leaves of varied tints,
Alone like some poor country lass
In th'house of a might prince.
Thus, I wandered in a crowd
Of hurrying, scurrying men;
Talking, jostling, noisy and loud
And looking now and then
At a man here or a girl there
With merely a passing glance
Each concern'd with his own affair
And his business life of Chance.
"Can "cars" make friends with me
Or the statue in the square,
Or the Thames, which rolls to th' sea,
Or Wandsworth's commons' fair?
Of City! – how I hate you,
You only stand and stare …
Have mercy when you view
This poor lone mortal's share."

Now, as a leaf I wander lone,
Or do I tell a lie?
The varied tints now seem to tone
And wind speaks with a sigh;
Here all the world is friendly
In this quaint old village place,
And folks they smile cheerfully
On a strange or unknown face.
They pass the time of day
These yeomen of this land
They guide you on your way
With Christian shake of hand.
Then out upon the highways

8

Where few folks seem to pass
'Good morrow friend' the robin says
 As he hops across the grass.
The country's friendly in a way
No artist can explain
The sweet perfume of new mown hay
The warm refreshing rain;
The measureless sky of azure hue
Sailed by countless clouds
Billowing sails an ocean of blue
With flapping wispy shrouds.
The stooks of kindly corn
Nodding their heads as they stand,
Glowing red gold at the dawn
Precious fruits of the land.
The chattering friendly brook
Talking all night and day,
Filling each cranny and hook
And gurgling on its way …
Thus nature proves to me
Its friendliness to man;
Since God has made it free
To aid his mighty plan.

April 1945

Victory in Europe Day

The day has come at least
For which we've waited long –
The dice has now been cast,
And Right has conquer'd Wrong.

We're happy now and wine flows free
As it did some years ago
They thought they end of wars they'd see
But blood still had to flow.

They mourn'd as we and danced as we
Lest we shall ere forget
Our children's children we must free
And those they shall beget.

They must not see the sights we know
Women and children killed –
Yet they should stand with heads bow'd low
Knowing how graves were filled.

Forgetting not what we have learnt
From blood and worry and sweat;
The ghastly grotesque forms of the burnt,
The corn fields stained and wet.

The ominous drone of approaching 'planes,
The death from the azure skies,
The men in prison camps in chains,
The worrying waiting wives.

As I write these words, I feel
They're cold and clearly set,
Thus when in prayer we kneel
God grant we'll ne'er forget.

May 1945

10

"To a Friend"

The finest things are worth so much
And yet they all are free;
But most of them we cannot touch
And few there are we see;
We feel the cool and gentle rain
We hear the birds of song,
We see the azure rolling main
The cedars tall and strong.
But, of the best, of all that's free
Is that which we shall never see,
The faithful bond of friend with friend
Which shall endure until the end
Because it's not of mortal kind
But betwixt the last mind.

June 1945

Comes the Dawn

Softly, silently, slowly revealing
Slips the night to the West receding
As on that far Eastern height
The sun stands up in a blaze of light.

The sins of the world with the night are gone
The sun comes up to lead us on;
The fields are clothed in emerald green,
And diamonds glisten where the dew has been.

The spiders web in the morning light
Is as faery lace spun in the night,
And mushrooms stand to tell the tale
Of faery feastings in the dale.

How I love to hear in the cool, fresh morn,
That song of the birds, greeting the dawn,
Those chattering sparrow in the eaves
That singing thrust amongst the leaves.

The sunlight steams thro' the pines on the hill
The copse is silent, fresh and still:
Then, in the scrub, a rabbit stirs
And birds fly out from the neighb'ring firs.

The whinnying horse from across the way –
The sonorous bell greeting the day …
Giving a message to all God's sons
From the swineherd's boy to the pious nuns.

Let all men marvel at the Dawn of Light,
When fresh hopes shine from out the night
For though that Night may swallow some …
The rest will stay till the race be run.

July 1945

Sarcasm?

You are cruel in your kindness to me
You are too fair in your justity
Your pleasantness is as a pleasantry;
Your faint praise too loud sounds,
It makes my deeds ring hollow:
A more glorious road, leaving thine to wallow
In the dust I've shaken to the ground.

October 1945

13

The Meteor

Men toiled
Horses stirred
The bridle rattled its tune,

Th' ploughshare cut
The soil turned
The sun was at its noon …

Autumn waited
The leaves fell
The shafts of the sun grew dim

A 'plane roared
The earth shuddered
The smoke was as black as sin …

A funeral pyre
Of white hot heat
Labourers rushed to the spot

Fire bells clanged
Sirens shrieked
But the flames they noticed not.

Sunset came
A sky of blood
The guard with bayonets stood

For 'neath the turf
A mortal lay,
At least, his mortal hood …

The dawn rose
On misty heights
The wreck lay, bare, forlorn.

Men lived;
But o'er the sea
Some women now will mourn.

Kimbolton, November 1945

The Canvas

How fresh art thou, clad in green,
Who wanders on this rural scene;
Who paintest all this pleasant land
With brush so gentle, so gentle hand …
Who breathes on it the breath of life
And setest all this place of strife
Alive! With many a bell
Or dainty foxglove in the dell.
The hedgerows burst with leafy flower,
And winter goes into her bower
For she doth fear this artisan
Whose work is praised by every man;
And whom the golden sun allies
To clear white winter from the skies.
Whose furtive fingers work unseen
Preparing vista's new and green;
Until with many parting tears
Spring leaves us as in bygone years.

Whilst as those tears refresh the earth
This land makes ready to give birth
To yet a more enhancing child
Whose hair is gold, and rather wild;
Who like a mighty enfilade,
Makes the green of cornfields fade
To now display in its ephemeral life
A field of golden glory – for the knife!
Oh virile child of Summertime
Heated devil of the pantomime,
Thou has burnt the very air
And mocked old winter in her lair;
But thy beast is yet too sure
For thou has now as ever more
Been overwhelming in thy heat
And none but thine own self doth cheat.

So now the wind with talons strong
Grasps the leaves as it stalks along

15

And mocks the trees so bold, yet bare
Which as a tonsured monk stand there
Defying still the hoary blast
Who on them scorning shrieking case

A force of elemental storm
Displayed in crafty cryptic form.
Though even still destruction bent
On autumn's task imperial sent;
You have that grain of good sown there
That even mortals seem to share;
And in titanic apparent rage
You leave behind the storm, you wage,
A field of gold strews in the wood
Where many may see that "God is good".

Bulbarrow Hill
March 1946

16

To the Sky

Inestimal beauty
Starry delight
Blue of the soul
My eyes alight
Tell of wonder
Oh exquisite eve,
Show to the world
The heavens believe
Enhancing and matchless
No canvas could touch
The immeasurable greatness
Of one who made such
Omnipotent reigning
Commanding the void
Nebulous glory
Of whiteness and froid,
Unhanded by men
Who puny and weak
Such incalculable wonder
Could never compete
Virginal other
Ordained unconquerable
Show us thy Maker
Almightily honourable;
King in the Highest
Designer Divine
Intangible hands
Inconceivably fine
Pearls in the carpet
Of regalist blues
Diamonds flashing
With countless hues,
Diaphanous clouds
Crossing the sky
Ethereal exuberance
Amazing the eye ....
Thine be the Glory
And Thine be the Praise,
Lauding eternal
To Thy Name we raise

May 1946

17

The Moon's Secret

As She gathered her skirts of light and left
Having danced all day in a golden dress
The last red ray swept away from the floor
And Night took her place in a sequined gown.
How gracious; gliding, she crosses the sea
Where a path of silver, shimmering light
Lies stretching far 'neath the alluring sky;
As over the mountains she dares to rise
Her dress cut low to show her creamy skin
Which, with enchanting beauty, holds spellbound
The very pulse of him who loves the day.
Her long black tresses on her shoulders lie,
Her face is radiance, sister to the day.
Her look is cold yet some refreshment brings
To tired souls who labour'd with the sun.
Is she not wondrous in her beauty, say,
Her form 'neath tulle sequined gown, so bold.
Those sequins shooting sparkling crystal darts
Lo, are they not numberless as the stars?
Her gown and hair, so black, ist as the Night?
And see her skirts fly wide and high about her,
As measureless as the mighty heavens?
Come, pray hold me not nescient of her name
Tis not fair to belie me further.   Stay,
Draw not a nebulous net before me
Let's hear her name, who owns the dress, the night,
For dalliance is her task, oh beauty bright!
'Oh damsel, mistress of mine, your name .....'
She answered not a word but danced away.

July 1946

18

Soliloquy on Truleigh Hill

Swish slips the grass by my trousers
Crunch crack the twigs 'neath my feet
I stride swiftly onward and upward
Enjoying the golden heat.
The air is clear …
So fresh up here …
And nature near …
How I love the drowsy heat.

In silent stillness snowswept slopes
Lonely as land could be
I was there with downcast hopes
Just the Downs alone with me.
In the Sun's pale glow
Which scarce can show
The shimmering snow
I stood with ice cold feet.

Squawk! … A flutter of wings!
A bird flies up from the ground …
And stay –
A nest I've found
As I walked with my eyes asleep …
How conscious of life I feel,
Its trials, its love, and its hate,
Of its tenderness too –
As I stare at the nest
Her achievement – those gems of blue.
Above the skylark hovers in the air
To sing his poets song.
There are crickets chirping in the grass
To help the world along
This day when the Prince is Spring
It's so good to be alive; …
But, out to sea, a cloud appears
And rain will rail the Prince …
Yet, another Spring will reign next year
And He will be just as young.

May 1947

For "Her"

Is not the glorious beauty of this radiant spring
A song with which our hearts should sing
Yet how, when many a pace
Lies there between you and this place,
How canst thou sing with me?

As dusk draws down her curtain o'er the fading day
And ont its velvet blue her stars display
I see Orion, hunter of the night,
Shining as tho' to put the moon to flight;
Look! You can see through window panes, the night as I,
The moon that doth upon the tree tops lie
Who casts her gentle garments in your room
Upon your bed the silent silver moonbeams strewn;
So over me, my face, and down the silent trees
She casts the self-same mantle with each case
That we, beneath that cloak, though far apart
Are close; reflected in her face ... your eyes, your heart.

The bluebells droop their heads and slumber 'neath the sky
The wood sleeps to the soft winds sigh
So I my bed must find,
And close the casements of my mind
To see you in my dreams –

May 1947

And why 'to War'?

Rearing rocks above splashing surf,
Heather'd heights o'er trespassing turf,
Mighty mountains stately standing.
Seagulls crying, circling, landing;
Tarns on hills, marsh in the glen
This is a land for men.
Here men toil and till the land
Here they work, and understand
The earth is a temple, the skies for a tent
The grass is its carpet, the flowers its scent;
The glorious purple enhanced with gold
The dewdrop diamonds which the sunlight hold,
Are gone in this place where man may dwell
Where he may draw form a living well
Of the highest thoughts that men require,
Those that are of Godly desire.
Loving one's land, and one's brothers too
Giving the world the best one can do.
This is the shape of the Craftsman' plan
Where man must work for the good of man.
By words alone man cannot live,
But from the fruit the field will give;
For by strong arms and heartfelt prayer,
The stones are bread and daily fare.
Thus when the golden grain turns black
And standing fields are beaten flat,
Though Moira may have set the sail,
Or Atropos with shears and scale
Done such as is beyond our ken …
We know not how, or why, or when?
Then, as a potter turns the clay
Events, as clay are turned His way;
Our empty barns turn their design
To other lands with another clime,
They hope for rich ripe corn do fill
Their empty sacks and disused mill.
Brotherly love on an ocean of strife,
Sharing the chart past the rocks of this life;
Whilst man fights wars he will fight again

For the blood to gush from another vein,
Whist the hydra grows another head
So women again will mourn their dead.
The bow is drawn across the strings
As though to draw the soul, on wings
From out Mars' trophies. Death transfixed
Friend and foe together mixed,
Is blood and mud the dead and living lie,
The stillness broken by the wounded's cry.
That cry which rends the temple veil
And rings o'er hill and quiet dale'
Which to the sleepy world inquiries;
"How can our God allow such fires
As these that are of evil fame,
Our men to kill, and blind and lame."
Still while the scarlet poppy grows'
Men struggle on with mortal blows.
But faithful we, should if we look,
See written in our Holy Book
That God still as a Father cares,
And give us of His Goodness shares …
For ever whilst blood still flows,
The poppy over Flanders grows.

February 1948

The Test Match Lament

In the hours of the Test
Hulton's thirty was our best
This may stir our Grace's rest
Sweet Spirit comfort him.

Fifty two a meagre score
Rather made the papers sore
"How", they said "the coaches swore!"
Sweet Spirit comfort them.

Win the toss – Invent the game!
Then to prove our 'sporting name'
Let the Aussies take the fame –
Sweet Spirit comfort us.

(Apologies to Robert Herrick – tho' I can't think why!)
Oval 1948

23

The Passage of the Years

With hurrying hand at chiming bell
Men mark the passage of the years,
And yet by these how can I tell
The joy prevailing thro' the tears?

If I but of your Thought could take a cup
And say "thus many times 'twas lifted up!"
I should your love to me have failed to show
For how could I account thy giving so?

Or, would that I could truly make
Reflected here in what you see,
The best which from yourselves you take
And freely offer unto me:

For, by an image such as this I'd show
(Whilst still confessing this the debt I owe)
What debt is here which never could be paid
Though honoured in, that it was ever made.

Therefore to you I pen this line
That: though imperfect it may be,
Yet shall you recognise the sign
Of gratitude expressed by me.

September 1949

Johnian Thoughts

How oft to these remembered walls
Have turned my waking thoughts, as falls
My step upon this well worn stone
That alma mater calls me home
To where I at sweet learnings breast
Have all my ignorance confessed.

Here stood in this familiar Court
And savoured of its secret thought
As I with your remembered sons
Well known and countless lesser ones
In Hall have read the grace before
Their few brief terms too quickly fly
As wind upon the Backs doth sigh
And gowned like I they wander by

Here as with Nash I saw the moon
Upon these Courts, her silver strewn
That cool and silent star stud sky
Wherein the aged secrets lie
And now as then despite the night
From many sets stream chinks of light.

Cambridge 1950

Saint Valentine's Day

Dearest, on my darling, were ever eyes so bright
Were ever lips so red, or skin so soft and white?
Was ever such a task to write of beauty rare,
To paint with wordy brush, a loveliness so fair?
Yet, you, before my eyes, these present moments show
Such beauty as no man has dared to dream to know.
So, trying not thy beauty to this page confine
I can but simply say to you "Will you be mine"
Because – I love you so ......

February 1950

26

Of "You and "I"

When shall this bloom yet blossom still more fair,
Or can this heart, too full, yet fuller be?
Can you, your face, your form, your fetching hair,
More lovely be the more of it I see?
Together, touching, can we closer be
And imitate the waves in their embrace;
Eternal, rising, surging as the sea,
Displaying strength; and gentle Beauty's face
When moonlit waves caress the quiet night:
Thus do we live, and treading virgin ways
Find yet still deeper depths and higher heights
In which our hearts may move throughout the days;
So greater joys for us shall still arise,
Since viewing each, we see though lovers' eyes.

April 1950

"Introversion" or "Conscience"!

How now, the gods have made a merry state'
For, with their blund'ring hand, which we call fate,
He that should thus their genius be
Must we call mad. For there we see
In him that should their wisdom show,
By his own mind, in argument to know
Between himself his mind divide,
And having fought in fight for either side,
Decree that by this twin cleaved brain
His 'inspiration', that's its name!
Is such that we who live in normal life
Know not the wisdom founded in such strife.
Thus, when we fondly say; "He is
But mad who eats his heart away
On problems of gargantuan size."
We know, that all the world is lies,
Since he who tears the mind he owns
Is not to madness gone;
But they who think it so.

April 1951

28

Of Love, or Retrospection

With bow bent full, that loosed shaft flow deep
Into the heart and mind that once was mine;
That heart is now for Thee, my pulses leap,
My mind no knowing has, save that for Thine.

Yet, shuttered from the world with whom I dwelt,
I anchored in the bay that was your Love
Plumbed deeper depths and sharper senses felt
Than dreamt I, in this world, a man could prove.

Yet, such is love; to know the hills of bliss,
Fond parting's tears, the new togetherness.
The upturned lip, the measure of our kiss,
The strength of life, the strange deep tenderness.

But then the paradox of love finds rest
In the etern'ty of Her lover's breast.

September 1951

29

London

Strange City of two thousand years
Who draws in mighty merchants trade,
How close the far-off shore appears
When , in thy breast, her wealth is made
The festive sport of tycoons play,
Who hold life's business to the glass
Make Business, Life and Work away
Whilst Beauty's sands too quietly pass.
What, though I know, from in Thy stones
A Kingdom's heart finds power to beat,
Yet from Thy stomach comes the moans
Of human brains, digested, meat
Crushed on Thy molar desks by day,
Then spewed out at night, along
The subterranean, swaying way
All jostling in the swirling throng,
And choking with Thy smoky breath
They flee the watchman's lamp before
And hurry home to Life, or Death,
Love, Hate or Pain within their door …
"Proud City, where's Thy shame tonight?"
Is it that bright and lurid light
Cloaked o'er the stones which Thou dost own;
Amid the stars of each man's home?

October 1951

Of Time's Duplicity

Our flower blossomed for one year
Then you, with partings sharp swift blade
Have sever'd that which was most dear,
And set aside the vows we made.

Distracted, and in foolish heart,
With memory's dew this twelve month past
In blossom rare, and kept apart,
This hothouse bloom was made to last.

But, as all flowers, it has died –
Though not forgotten, yet, unmourned.

July 1952

The Cruise

Though mine, I sail a wanton vagrant yacht
Who pulls so hard the hands that check her sheets
Or heels, so to the strong winds eye she beats
And chuckling onto crested wavelets top.

At night, she rides the shimm'ring murky deep
Her mast probing excited starry space;
Her decks, all dewy, hold the pale moon's face
And, restlessly, she rocks our dreams to sleep.

Yet mine, she carries one I would were mine,
For here we slept so close, but did not touch
We were so near, and yet, our hearts as such
Did never love, and do not now entwine.

Norfolk
September 1952

32

The Seagull

See here the sun breaks though the misty morn
And Thames' breath subdues the man made scene
A steely forest, derricks, cranes, forlorn
Which by the moving murky waters lean.

Here massive buildings crowd the muddy shore
And on the backcloth, faint, ethereal drawn
The Tower, reflects as in Time's mirror'd door
A warning to the Bridge's slothful yawn.

And here, across the spanning bridge, you see
A myriad of your makers, chained to you
Who move beneath that Seagull, flying free
And see in him, their souls fly free and true.

So, swooping, soaring, cleaving through the air,
"Finds your white body joy, and freedom, there?"

London Bridge
December 1952

33

Whilst returning Home

The feathery fingers finely traced
Against the redd'ning West,
The spacious blue,
Of the sunset's rays
And the shades, as the day seeks rest.

A crystal star in the high deep sky
Calls on the faithless moon
The sharp black house
And the lazy smoke
Fade, in my sight, too soon.

The soft wet turf and the warm south wind
Together give new life
My heart awakes
And my soul
Is touched, after the City's strife.

Chipstead Golf Course
February 1953

The Voyage

We seek not what we know
But striving still
Our questing souls pursue a chartless way;
Across unending seas
We move
And turn not back.

Surely sweet muse can tell
Or prophet point my way –
Ambition be my goad or guide
Or gentleness, or grace
Redeem my day.

Yet seek a kingdom here?
Or plan a guileless home?
Stay, watch the others on their way
Or seek a secret cell,
Find lowliness or fame
But find, and know, the way ….

Ah! There's perplexity
For who can say (for me)
The Here, or Now
Or be the light on which to point ambition's prow.

And yet the hands of older men can point
Or be upheld;
And I can sup upon sweet learning's milk, and know:
Yet greater freshment can I find
For out religious jagged rock, can flow
A healing water and the peace of mind:
Besides, dear hands can seek for mine
And loving eyes
Say all the man can need to know.

1954

Gibraltar

Within our home
May hearts enfold
And in Gibraltar peace
Forever hold
The love that I renew this day
Which is for you and is for aye
Bright in sweet Sussex shine
A beacon for our children and our time,

Gibraltar Farm
Firle, Sussex

11th October 1958 - 1979

Ladies Livery

As Aphros from the sea was made
From petalled bosom's blue brocade
Rise perfect (as you cast your cape)
'Your creamy shoulders' lovely shape;
And so you glide with measured tread
Still, vainly do, your roses red
Outbid the beauty given you
Of lips as fresh as morning dew –
Here round us marble maidens stand
In Drapers; Hall, neath painters' hand
Unsmiling canvas kings look down
And wish away the royal crown …
To live, on this especial day
When you to Beauty's self display
A manifest, of all their dreams ….
And mine -

Drapers' Hall 1959

37

Armistice memorial in today's world

Saturday night and the same again
I loved her then as I love her now
Bird I said what the hells your name
You're a Saturday moll lets do it again
Its no good crying to Mum and Dad
Who the hell cares now as we roll again
Love I said its always the same.

As a kid I heard of the knight and the maid
Striving for love and finding it made
But not on earth its always the same –
Well a new bints fresh but only in name.

Lets break their self destroying role
Of useless loves without a goal
Whether shes virgin whether shes whore
I cant get fulfilment – not evermore.
Either its her or maybe its me
Whose the exploited we'll never agree –
Pathetic she lies on her back with her fag
May be that it – I try a new drag
And ride on a star – the trip of my life
Wow now we're away and leaving the strife.
Boy fabulous here to weave in the air
Weightless seeing her beauty so fair
A sense of fulfillment but only for now
The walls are so heavy they're crushing us now
I surface, I gasp, cry out for a breath
I'm shaking and stricken and staring at death
Still lacking the weed has no thrill anymore
How was it Blake had the vision he saw
I'll try for a fix
Mutual indulgence –
Its only for kicks!
My self is still sadder
I yearn for repose
And crave some purpose
In being, God knows.

This trip will be best
I'm off on my tod …….
The box is packing music
And the pitch is mighty fine
I see the people of the world
Upon its muddy face

38

And these that love like I have done
Are lost without a trace
But those who offer first themselves
With dignity find love –
The other sod's a person –
Not an object without face
A soul that yearns for being
And a heart in search of grace
Yep, I see most all the people
In the self same noose as me
Their relationships exploit them
And expose them to frustration
in the vort of misery.

Now the fix is nearly ended
And the visions fading fast
I hear the Angels singing
Is this heaven itself at last?
The walls stretch into darkness
And they run with blood so red
He says its poppy petals
Who's this voice from out the dead
It all sounds strange but magic
And the trumpet thrills my veins
He says they've solemn faces
And the medals flash with light
Again there comes the vision
Of a heavenly angel bright
Is this winged Angel death
Or Victor in the mud of Mons
Did they who live and they who died,
Find peace in service side by side –
Like a tide of restless faces, They sing
The organ peels again
A strange triumphant hymn
Their faces hold fulfillment
Of valiant heart they sing.

Now the squares and rounds dissolve
In trembling sweat I live
I see with new born eyes
The love that satisfies
They gave themselves
The essence of the God made man
To give not get my life must be
To find the love that sets me

11.11.1964

Peterbu – Danebu

Oh silent world we hear you
Quietness in the evening time
And here hot noon day sun
Is cold beside the fire bright pine

In lake of liquid freshness here we bathe
The cool cleanness of its fresh dark depths
The languid drooping fir trees wave
As on the mountain face we climb.

Peace rippled by the trout plucked flies
From evenings warm south western breeze
A cow bell echoes through the trees
And in the summer stillness no bird cries.

Darkness if not a part
Of this light midnight world
Were watchful mornings summer light
Shines over Norway's ridged and vallied heart.

Sweet other worldliness of Summer here
Where all the rocks prepare for snow
The deep and winter solitude
Which even here in summer is the gift of Peterbu.

Aurdal Norway
1970

The Fortunate Isles

White flecked the waves from Tean
Licks across the bay
Soaring like Easter gulls
On this all joyous day –
Man's soft green turf slopes gently down
Beneath the heathers wastes to old church town
The glorious sun that pierces sharp tongued wind.
Down smugglers path, on past the school
From Grimsbys o'er the hill
Down meadow land and past the golden gorse
The people come to sing for joy
The isles of peace and liberty galore
Gives Love and Peace and Awe.

Easter Day (JJ Birthday)
Tresco 1974
Isles of Scilly

The Electronic Age

We with the science of the years
Distill sweet knowledge
For the forward way
And rearrange the moments to find forms
A binal pulse stores knowledge
In lectronic brains
And thermal nuclear alterations give us power
But all we have is change
Though not one neutron have we gained
The metamorphous of our sphere
Is known as "wisdom" and energy unleashed for strength
What gain have we in charity or love.

The City desk
London 1982

42

Time Past

Time past needs not this written line –
For here tomorrow lies asleep, and may be
For future's not alone the day determined
But the gift of Fortune's wheel.

Alone 'the day that was' in mine to hold
and not forget.
Or cast aside into the sea of 'not-to-be remembered' past
So as the swan from out the gloom
of murky rivers drabness
Whiteness and beauty come unsought.

There needs no memory's cell to hold –
For fast upon the living self remains
The days remembered.

Those eyes that hold the joy of spring
and laughing,
Keep in check the warmth of Summer's Sun
The self that swan like is both strong and soft
of regal bearing and a homeliness.

A daughter, proud and yet a loving child at heart
Ah, there's the clue –
In all uncertain life the present and the past is yours
The future yet to take.

No man can say for you
Nor Priest or Parent guide that choice
Alone to each decide ......
if this be Love.

Are these the dreams that are more real
The more of them we see?
Or do they turn to dust and crumble with the break of day?
Are we .... but that's for you to say
The truth like love is hard to know
And if we seek too hard it may be lost
For happiness is given never found –

Firle 1984

A Firle Carol written for the Sixth Viscount Gage

Christmas is dawning,
Like the first morning,
Children are singing
Like the first day.
Let me too praise him,
He who is coming,
Each new renewing
Upon our way.

God is descended
Into each person,
Born in all people
As he first came.
Open your ears then
Like Mother Mary
To angels singing
Glory God's name.

Open your eyes then
As did the sages
To God's great riches
Given for men.
Then let your lips sing
As did the shepherds
Telling of God's peace
Sent now and then.

Thus may we echo
God's new beginning
Offered to all men
Each glad new day
Death, life and rebirth,
His re-creation,
Sing down the ages
Truth is for aye.

Victoria Hospital 1985

Vasiliko at Dawn

Was ever world so still
Clouds in seas at dawn
Ripples twist, and clearly seen
Rusty anchors in tiny forest of kelp
The minnows in their secret world
Hurrying they only know to where
Orange and blue the caiques sleeps on
Their props of trees. White hulled
She sorts the yellow nets;
With grey and black of youth, generations all
The family together unravelling the tangle of timelessness
And one more day so many others
But one new precious moment of time like no other
Never repeated yet constant
Continuing begins this happening of stillness.

Greece 1985

45

The Children's Hope

The psychiatric cry is love the young
For this gives balance to the mind?
So we must first be wraught in them
Then for their world
An equanimity we find
No man can hold eternal life
We cannot save from fire or sword
Yet giving love, we give the strength beyond ourselves
To hold our sons, when we are gone
To lift them up unto the Sun.

Firle 1986

Kornate Archipelago

Jadron so deep so blue
Show us the pearl we seek of you
As swiftly on your moving face
Appears our creamy wake
And far behind
Long lines the endless repetition make
Hot sun and clearness here
Brown skin to greet the wanderer.

Yugoslavia 1986

A Downland Idyll

Out of the swirling galaxies of gasses moving but immovable in the mists of time I am part of immortality the spark of the infinite an all seeing eye of the all seen and I yearn to know those who live, albeit temporarily, outside this constance space in the confines of time itself.

The energy that is the Creator that is beauty, truth and strength combined knows all, sees all, understands all but with infinite gentleness and compassion hopes for the redemption of all those locked outside of immortality.

I must go for you and see for myself, I must dive as a hawk seeing both the great expanse and yet picking out the tiniest shrew running between the standing corn.

I will focus from that realm which needs no focus down into time itself and see how those enslaved by its moving hands have understood anything of that immortality which is to be or simply laboured for that hour which exists.

Hurtling through that impossible barrier which is time itself on which is rent only by what mortals call death, my hurtling vision focused on a thousand years which are as nothing but I saws in them a Downland Sanctuary and from it came yearnings of immortality over all the hours and days of those thousand years.

Praise was given to the Creator who is forever, favour beseeched, promises made, and confessions unburdened.

Surely in that brief span and in the still briefer lives that are the seconds of the minutes and the minutes that are the years of the hour that are the century's I saw joy and happiness all that is good and beautiful and I saw sadness for of that is mortality made and not the infinite love of the infinite truth that is of all time.

I am a traveller in time and I see a sanctuary that strives to be beyond time and the sanctuary is a people and within people and it is here as I see the hidden green waves on the Sussex downs.

Firle 1989

48

Firle Beacon

The blush of dawn suffused the night clouds frown
As gentle morn came rolling o're the downs
As soft as wavelets on the mornings shore
And earth was yet more lovely then before.

Ascension Day 1998

49

A Birthday Thought

Marked down the ages
Stand the monuments of men
Faint aspiration to an immortality
Within the changing years
We have no need of Mecca
Or the pharaohs sphinx
There is no scared spot
Save in the heart
No proof by things or gifts
Only the knowledge that is true
And truth is now
And of all time.

Of what is past remember hours of ease
Lights rippling on the mirrored waters darkened face
A country walk when spring gave freshness to the air
And then the age old inn when twilight burnished sun has reddened
all the sky.

These hours and a host beside
Gay laughter and the chink of glass
Within the social whirl
Or when the hooves were thudding on the turf
External moments when an organ breathed Bach's magic in the air.

Firle
10.09.2003

50

Armada Anniversary Sunday

In this sanctuary has trembled a spark breaking out as a star in eternity, and in this timelessness the voice of Firlemen say with the Psalmist voice of three thousand years ago, 'The lot has fallen on to me in a fair ground, Yea I have a godly heritage.'

Climb we the Ancient Downland ways
Where our Stone Age fathers trod.
Seek in the rolling Sussex Downs
The hidden greenways of God.
Lift our eyes to the strong smooth hills
encircling our homes and lives;
Here is peace and strength to our wills,
And a love that never dies.

Sunrise, sunset, red gold, the sky.
Raised over sacred Barrows
A beacon of light from on high.
The plough turning life's furrows
As it strikes on the flints of time;
We glimpse in Armada fires.
A burning bush and Holy Sign.
The spark of the Light Divine.

Safe in the arms decreed by time.
Black Cap Down to Caburn Mount
This village lies, a timeless sign.
Of our loving God the found
Of living waters flowing true;
Life to sheep and golden grain,
Springs from the wells of downland dew
Our souls washed with Holy Rain.

Now, thank the Lord God who made us
To dwell in this pleasant land.
Raise thankful hearts for the blessings
Received from His generous hand.
Climb we the ancient Downland way
Where our stone age fathers trod.
Seek in the rolling Sussex Downs.
The hidden greenways of God.

Read by Canon J Woodward
Firle Church. 1988

51

Printed in Great Britain
by Amazon